IF AT FIRST YOU DON'T SUCCEED…

Donald Gorbach

Copyright © 2017 by Donald Gorbach

All rights reserved.

ISBN:1977744109
ISBN-13: 978-1977744104

"IT'S FINE TO CELEBRATE SUCCESS BUT IT IS MORE IMPORTANT TO HEED THE LESSONS OF FAILURE"

-BILL GATES

REALITYCOVERBOOKS.COM

www.ingramcontent.com/pod-product-compliance
Lightning Source LLC
Chambersburg PA
CBHW050214230526
45470CB00001B/376